Little Scientists, BIG Questions

What Does a Dentist Do?

Written and Designed by Alix Wood

WINDMILL BOOKS

Published in 2025 by Windmill Books,
an Imprint of Rosen Publishing
2544 Clinton St.
Buffalo, NY 14224

Cataloging-in-Publication Data

Names: Wood, Alix.
Title: What does a dentist do? / Alix Wood.
Description: Buffalo, New York : Windmill Books, 2025. | Series: Little scientists, big questions
Identifiers: ISBN 9781538395363 (pbk.) | ISBN 9781538395370 (library bound) | ISBN 9781538395387 (ebook)
Subjects: LCSH: Dentists--Juvenile literature. | Dentistry--Juvenile literature.
Classification: LCC RK63.W66 2025 | DDC 617.6--dc23

Image Credits:
Science Photo Library: 14 (Zephyr); Shutterstock: Cover (Drazen Zigic), 3T (Alongkorn Sanguansook), 4 (Roman 3dArt), 5 (DuxX), 6 (Edvard Nalbantjan), 7T (sirtravelalot), 7B (Maksym Bondarchuk), 8 (Wavebreak Media), 9T (Maxx-Studio), 9B (Inside Creative House), 10 (gomolach), 12 (Alex Mit), 13 (Dmitry Naumov), 15 (Svitlana Hulko), 16T (Crime Art), 16B (Alex Mit), 17 (Alex Mit), 18T (M2020), 18B (Alex Mit), 19T (Ross Helen), 19B (Dmitry Naumov), 20T (tinglee1631), 20B (sirtravelalot), 21 (Sen. Sever/P Maxwell Photography/Anton Starikov/Sashkin/M. Unal Ozmen/Bigmouse 108/Andrey Kuzmin/Enlightened Media/Hong Vo/vipman/CWIS/Pixfiction), 22 (B Bernard), 23T (Macrovector); Superstock: 11 (Lewis Houghton/Science Photo Library); Alix Wood/Ruby Tuesday Books: 2–3.

Printed in the United States of America

CPSIA Compliance Information: Batch #CSWM25
For Further Information contact Rosen Publishing at 1-800-237-9932

Find us on

Today, we are visiting the dentist.

Next patient please!
Dr. O. Penwide
It's my turn next!

Dentists help people keep their teeth, gums, and mouths healthy.

They have to learn lots of facts about teeth.

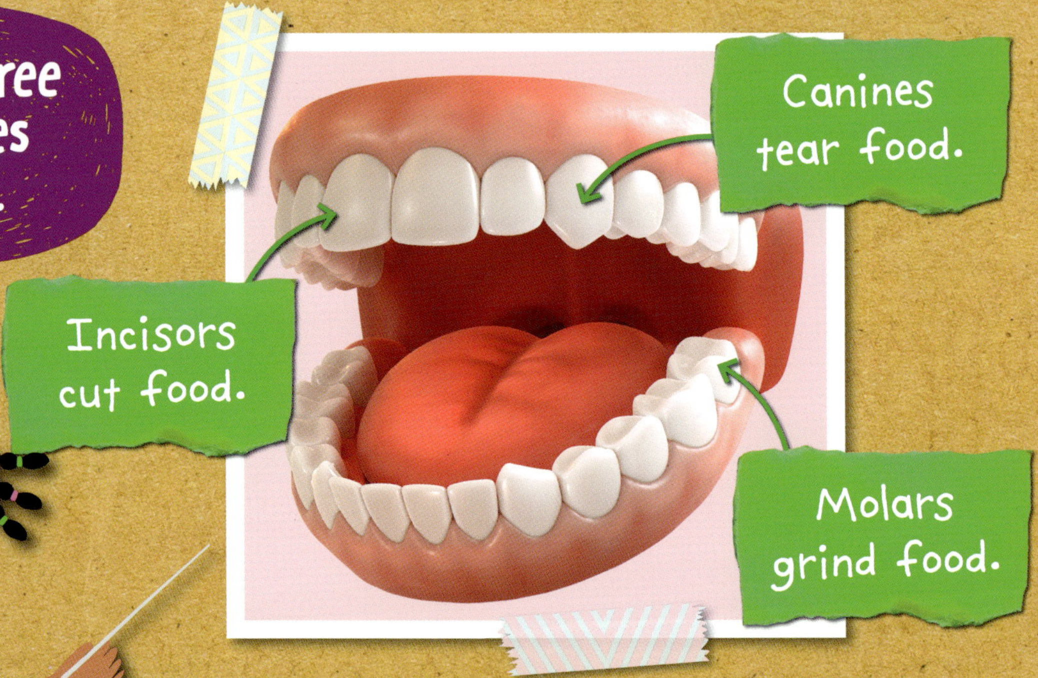

Teeth are covered in superhard enamel. Enamel is the hardest part of a person's body!

Dentists use science to do their job.

Come on, little scientists, let's answer that BIG question!

A dentist works in a room called an exam room.

The patient sits in a BIG chair.

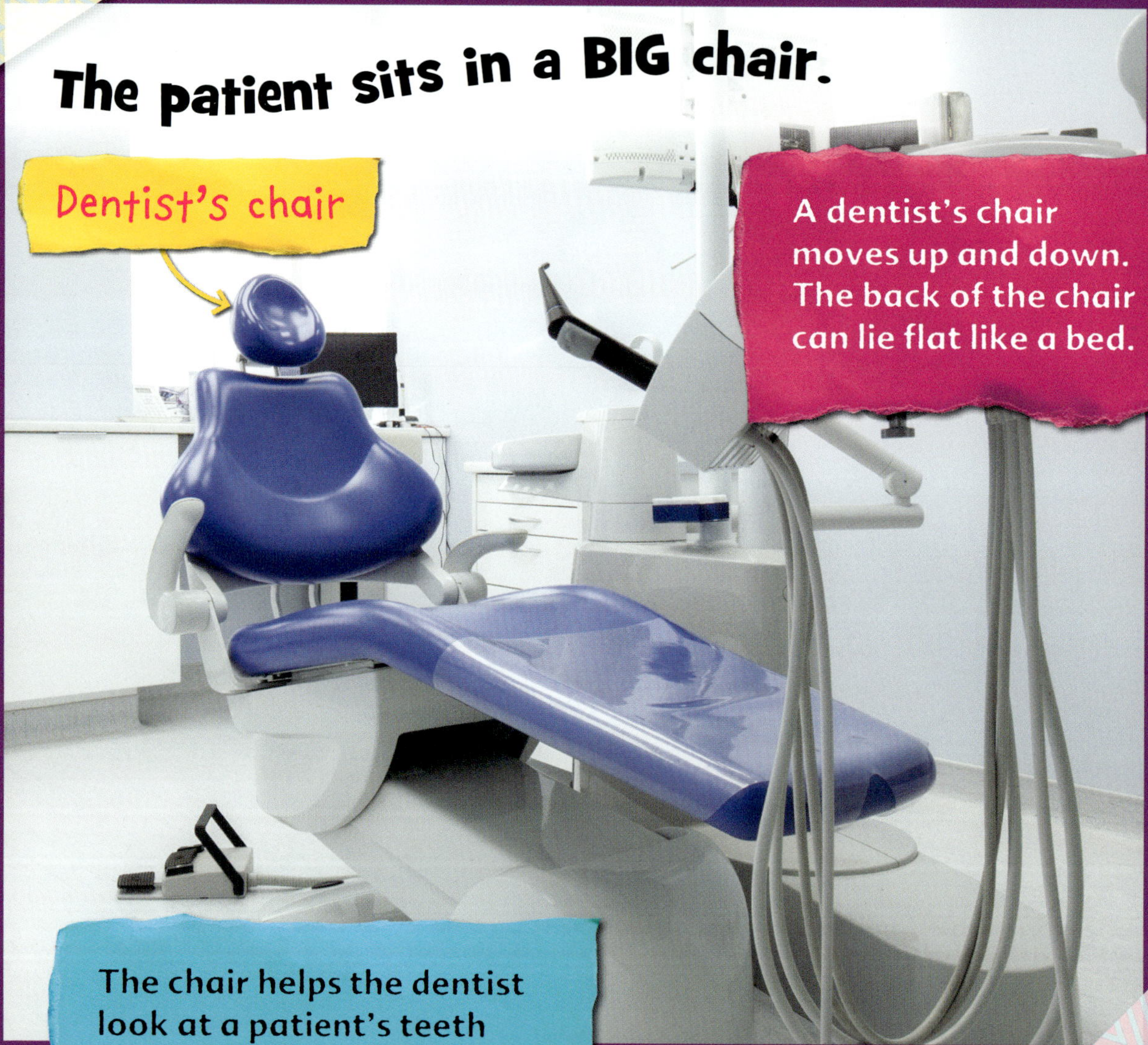

A dentist's chair moves up and down. The back of the chair can lie flat like a bed.

The chair helps the dentist look at a patient's teeth from different angles.

A dental assistant helps the dentist.

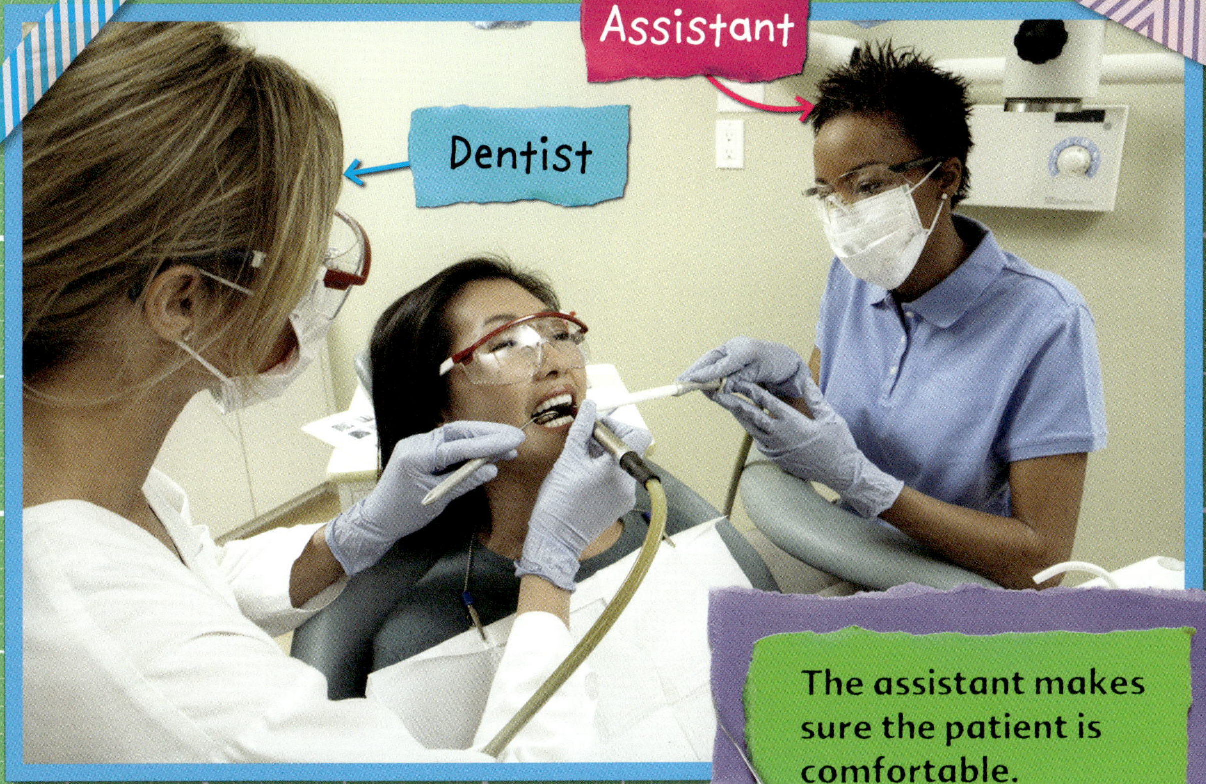

The assistant makes sure the patient is comfortable.

They pass the dentist the tools they need.

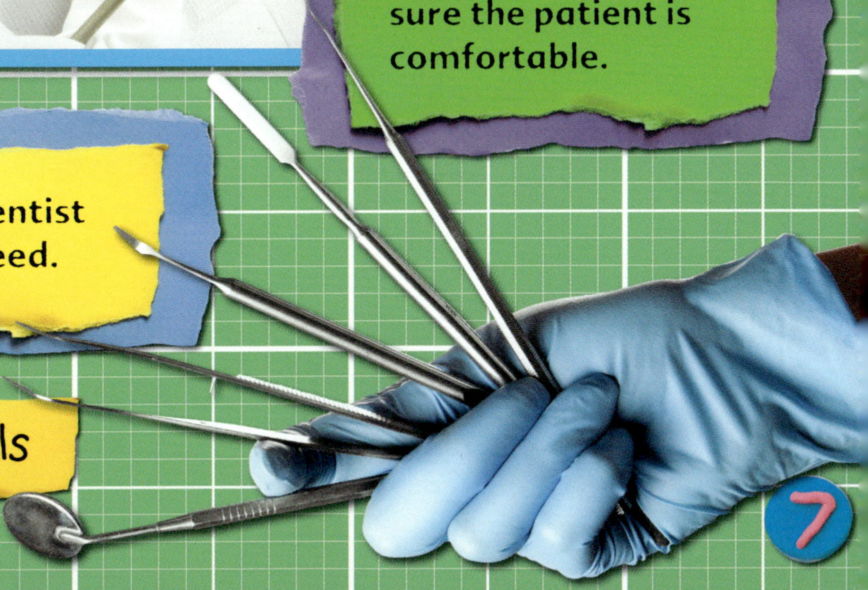

Dental tools

Time for a Checkup!

The dentist shines a bright light in the patient's mouth to check the teeth.

Sometimes, the patient wears protective glasses.

Our mouths are home to tiny living things called bacteria.

When bacteria and bits of food mix together, they make a sticky covering called plaque.

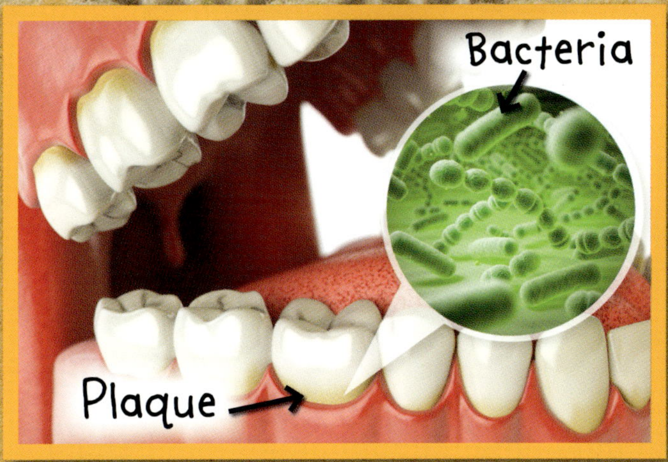

The dentist uses a mirror on a stick to look all around each tooth.

Plaque can damage your gums and cause tooth decay.

At the dentist, each tooth is given a number.

As the dentist checks a patient's teeth, they say different numbers.

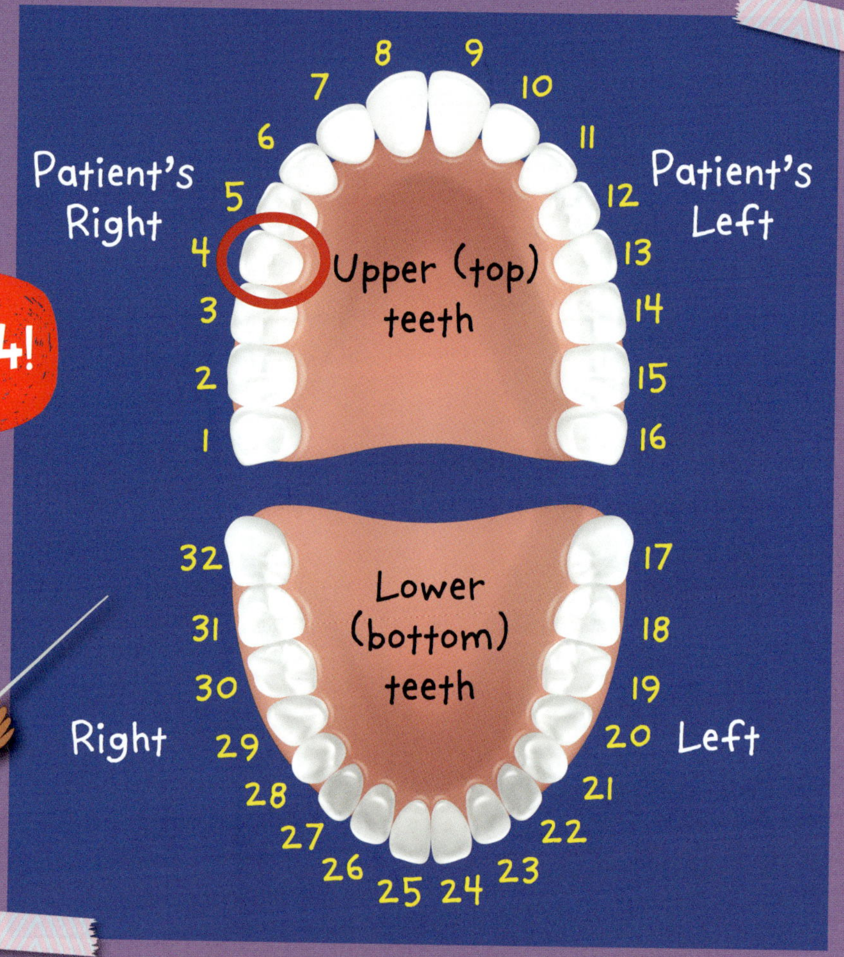

"Number 4" means the fourth tooth from the back on the upper right side of the jaw.

The numbers are like a dentist's code. They describe each tooth and its gum.

The assistant types the information into a computer.

The code helps the dentist keep a record of each tooth.

Sometimes a dentist uses an X-ray machine to take a picture of a person's teeth.

X-rays are pictures of what's inside a person's body.

Bones and teeth show up brightly on an X-ray picture.

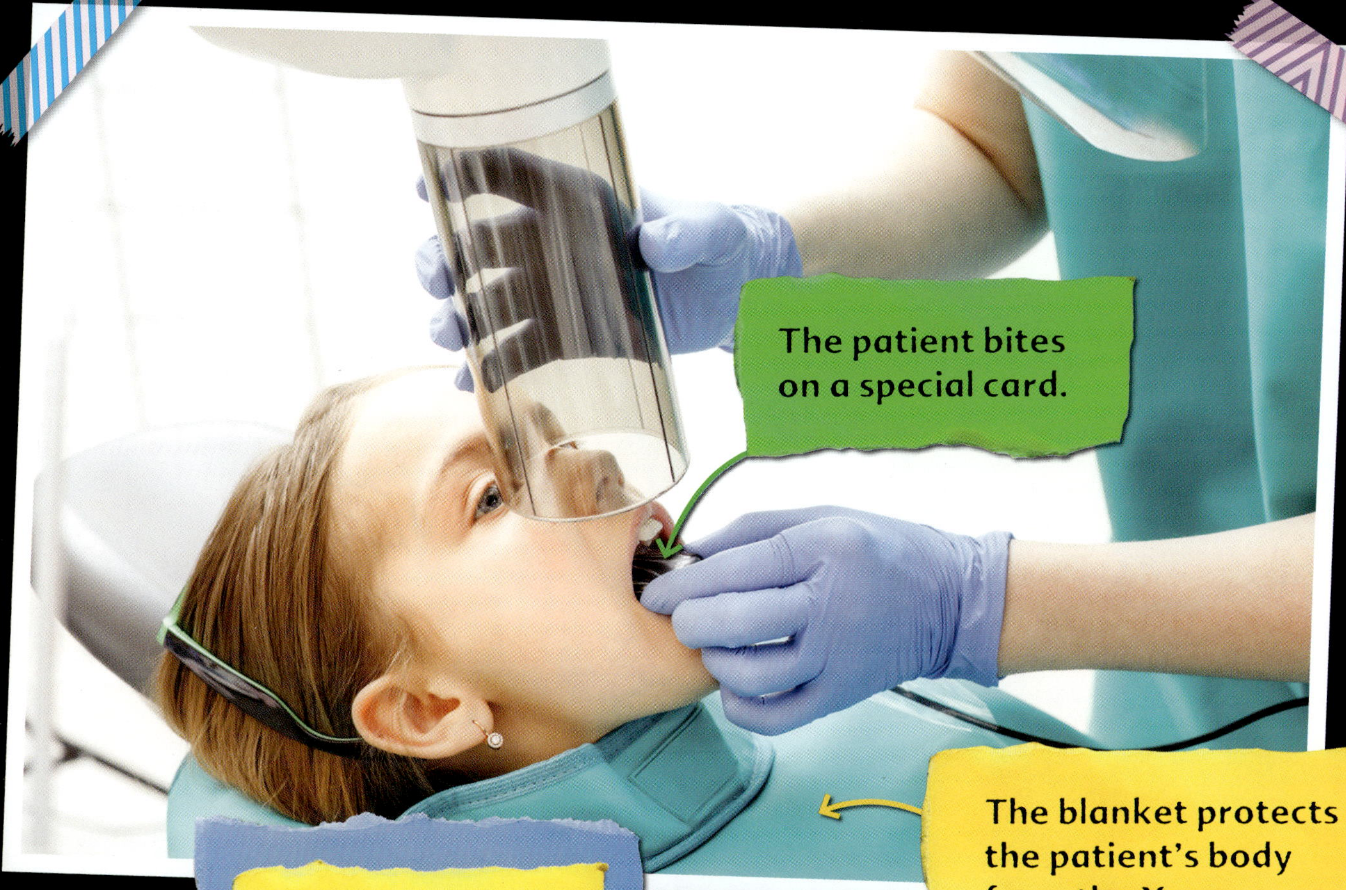

X-rays can show problems in your bones, teeth, and gums.

An X-ray can show that a patient has a small hole in their tooth. The hole is called a cavity and it can be painful.

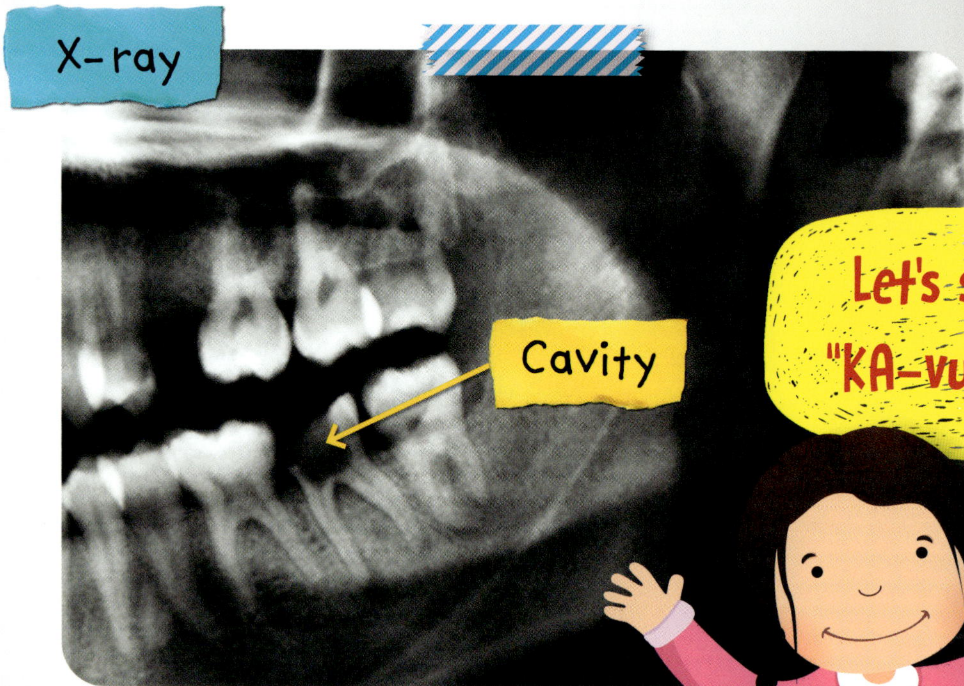

Tooth decay makes the hard enamel on teeth get softer. Then a person may get cavities.

A dentist uses science to fix a cavity!

First, the dentist gives the patient a special injection in their gums so they won't feel pain.

The injection is an anesthetic that makes the patient's mouth go numb.

Let's say it!
"a-nis-THEH-tik"

What happens next to fix a cavity?

The dentist uses a tiny drill to remove decaying, or bad, parts of the tooth around the cavity.

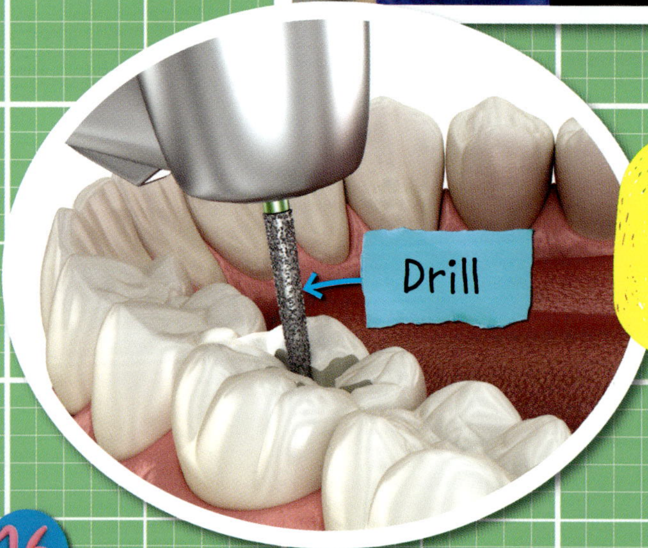

Then the dentist fills the hole with strong material that hardens.

A dentist can give a person's teeth a great cleaning!

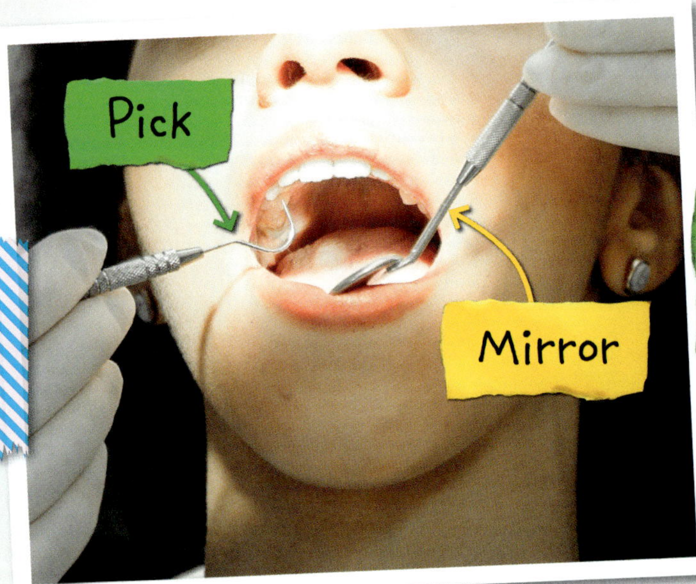

Sometimes a tooth expert called a dental hygienist does this.

The dentist removes stuff called tartar with a tiny pick.

When plaque hardens, it forms yellow tartar.

The dentist also removes plaque and tartar with an electric scaling tool.

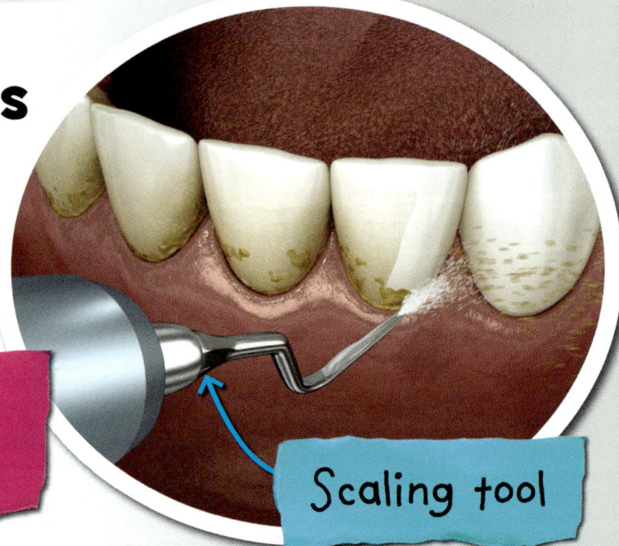

Water blasts from the tool.

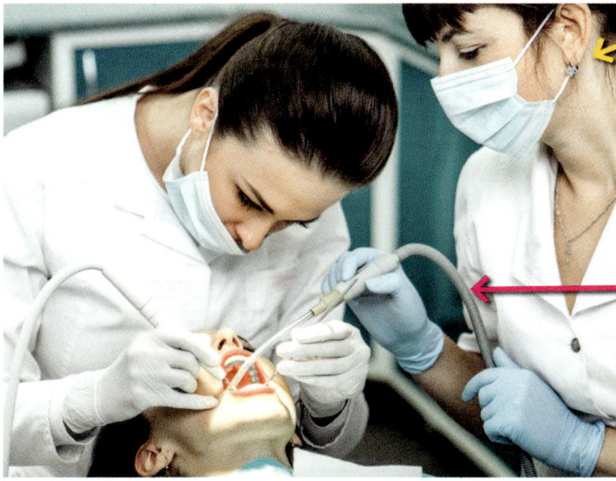

Assistant

This tube sucks up water and bits of tartar.

Finally, the dentist polishes the teeth.

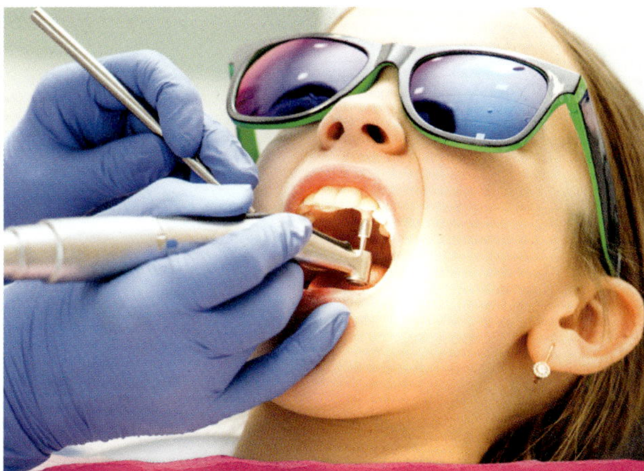

It's harder for plaque to stick to smooth, polished teeth.

Now my teeth are smooth and shiny!

Dentists teach us how to keep our teeth healthy.

This helps prevent toothaches, tooth decay, and cavities.

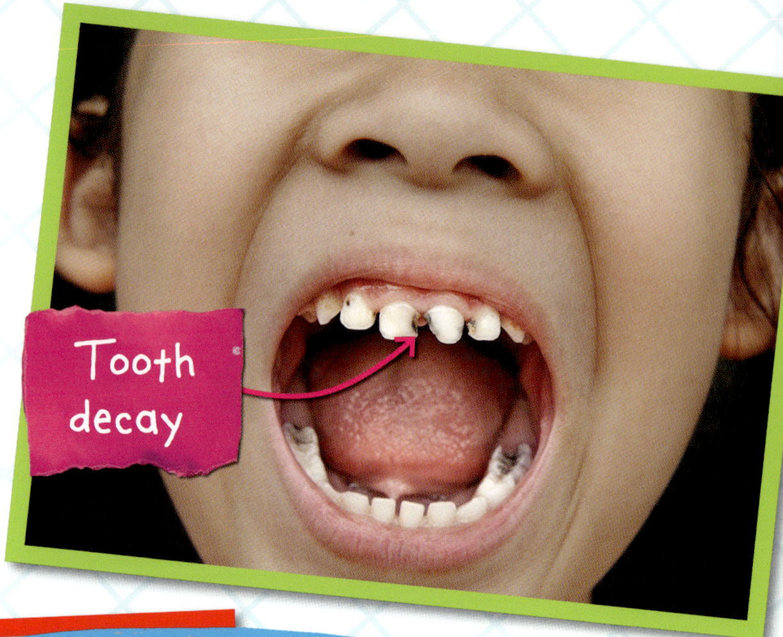

Don't drink sugary drinks.

Don't eat too many sugary foods.

Bad for teeth

Good for teeth

Bacteria love sugar! They feed on sugary foods and drinks that stick to your teeth.

That's why it's important to brush your teeth!

Brush your teeth twice every day for 2 minutes each time.

Make sure one of your brushing times is before bed.

There's special stuff called fluoride that protects our teeth.

Fluoride is found in toothpaste. It helps strengthen the enamel on your teeth and stops tooth decay.

Let's say it!
"FLOR-ide"

Now we know how dentists use science. Good work, little scientists!

My Science Words

cavity
A hole in a tooth that forms when a person has tooth decay.

enamel
The hard outer layer of your teeth.

plaque
A soft, sticky covering on teeth that is always forming. Brushing your teeth removes plaque.

tooth decay
Damage to your teeth that can make cavities and give you a toothache.